FACETS OF LIFE

Pookie's Poetry

SHERMAN L. FOWLER

 FriesenPress

Suite 300 - 990 Fort St
Victoria, BC, V8V 3K2
Canada

www.friesenpress.com

ISBN
978-1-5255-8959-1 (Hardcover)
078-1-5255-8958-4 (Paperback)
978-1-5255-8960-7 (eBook)

1. POETRY, AMERICAN, AFRICAN AMERICAN

Distributed to the trade by The Ingram Book Company

TABLE OF CONTENTS

INTRODUCTION

In 2008, Sherman L. Fowler, former Parent Coordinator of East St. Louis School District 189, was named Cambridge Who's Who Professional of the Year in Parent-Student Coordination. Inclusion in the Cambridge Who's Who Registry is an honor, and only a small selection of members in each discipline are chosen for this distinction. These special honorees are distinguished based on their professional accomplishments, academic achievements, leadership abilities, years of service, and the credentials they provide.

With more than thirty-five years of professional experience, Fowler specialized in photography and developing lead parent programs. At his previous post, he was responsible for conducting computer classes, seminars, and workshops for parents, auditing operations for all schools. In addition, he implemented the No Child Left behind Act and served as a liaison between several communities in coordinating an annual community fair. He previously worked as a communication and media technology instructor at the University of Jos, Nigeria, and as an instructor at Obafemi Awolowo University, Ile Ife, Nigeria.

A published poet, Fowler co-authored a book entitled *Visible Glory: The Million Man March* with Eugene B. Redmond and Marcus Atkins. His poetry has been published in Black World, *Sides of the River, Break Word, Black Literature Forum, Drum Voices Revue, Literati Chicago, East St. Louis Monitor* and Other publications, including audio and video recordings. He has performed his poetry in such venues as churches, schools, street corners, radio, television, pubs, clubs, parties, and campuses. He was presented With a Community Fair Award in 2008, was inducted into the Freelance Photographers Hall of Fame in 2008 and Poetry Hall of Fame in 2005, and is recognized by Who's Who in Photography.

Fowler received his Master's Degree in Education in 1976 and his Bachelor's Degree in Communication In 1972 from Southern Illinois University. He is a co-founder of the Eugene B. Redmond Writers Club and a member of the International Society of Poets and the International Freelance Photography Association. His affiliation with the EBR Writers Club and his personal travels have allowed him to Associate with Henry Dumas, Katherine Dunham, Amiri Baraka, Margret Walker Alexander, Quincy Troupe, Gwendolyn Brooks, Walter Mosley, Jayne Cortez, Eugene B. Redmond, Mari Evans, Haki Madhubuti, John Figueroa, Raul Salinas, James David Rubadiri, Shirley Bradley Le Flore, Michael Castro, Maya Angelou, Wole Soyinka, Chinua Achebe, Akinsola Akiwowo, and many other writers, musicians, actors, and educators.

His wife, Harriette B., aka "Peaches", joined the ancestors in 2016 after forty-nine years of marriage They had become residents of Atlanta, GA, after Fowler retired in 2009. Fowler's poetry has been described as pictures painted with the words of a spiritual warrior that speak to and for new-world Africans; his weapons are love, joy, peace, wisdom, knowledge, and understanding, and he protects his world with truth.

Facets of Life is profound. Reboot your thinking machine, take a soul-trek with Pookie to the rainforest of immeasurable enlightenment, where an indivisible love-being reigns supreme.

Note: You can contact Sherman by email, shermanfowler@outlook.com, and for information about Kwansabas, contact: eredmon@siue.edu.

Sherman L. Fowler, AKA Pookie,
and Harriette B. Fowler, AKA Peaches.

PROLOGUE: FACETS OF LIFE

Summary

Sherman L. Fowler Radio Interview on
Tokovlradio with Radio Personality
Renee A. Johnson (LadyRaeJ)
May 25, 2020

Sherman L. Fowler, also known as "Pookie," is an African American
hall of fame poet who was the protégé of the late poet Henry Dumas.
He co-authored a book, *Visible Glory: The Million Man March*, with
Dr. Eugene B. Redmond and Marcus Atkins. Co-founder of the Eugene
B. Redmond Writer's Club, along with Eugene Redmond and Darlene
Roy, his poetry appears in many magazines and anthologies.

If I were asked to describe Sherman L. Fowler in one word, it would
be thoughtful! Being thoughtful in his manner of expression through
poetry, Sherman has the ability to paint pictures with words that
dance off the page and onto the canvas of the mind! When I asked
Sherman how he came to write poetry, he stated: "It was really four
of us when we started off back in the sixties: Joseph Harrison, who
passed away from illness; Henry Dumas, who was my mentor; and
Eugene Redmond, who was also a mentor. We all used to hang out
together, and Gene and Henry Dumas brought me out of the poetic
closet, because all I did was write poetry in a book and kept it there."

I went on to say, "It [poetry] makes you really think about how you
view yourself, how you view the world, and how you view yourself
in the world, particularly with, 'Check Out Your Mind,' because that
poem seems to be one that addresses the making of a slave."

Sherman agreed. "Yes, that is what conquerors do. They acculturate,
they assimilate, and they colonize minds. They make you like them,
and that is what has occurred with African Americans. The people

that they brought here to this country, we were never slaves. We were kidnapped victims."

Where would we be if these works of poetic art had stayed locked away from the light of day? Thankfully, we will never know! I have fallen in love with this form of poetic gesture again, because there is so much history and culture embraced in the way Sherman talks about things in life that shape us into who we have become as living, breathing beings.

Sherman has had the privilege to have been taught by some very notable influencers in our society of art and poetic expression. I felt like I was being told about relatives of my very own family when he spoke of the teachings in his life as a poet. In his poem, "Black History Yesterday and Today," we discussed how black history of yesterday is still black history of today. Sherman spoke very candidly about that.

"Well, it has changed the interaction of African Americans. This is why they keep trying to keep us separate from them, because they have classified us as less than human. And if we interact with them, they can get to realize we are not different from any other human being; all human beings are human beings. There are good human beings; there are bad, stupid human beings. People who behave stupidly... I'll say it, that some people are intellectually brilliant because they develop themselves to that degree. They are no smarter than anybody else. They just work at whatever, being intelligent, knowing, and understanding things. They work at it. It's ... it's an exercise of mind."

I talked further on this topic, due to the intense racial tension of our country in 2020, by mentioning one of his mentors, Henry Dumas: "You address, in your poem about 'Black History Yesterday and Today' that your mentor, the poet Henry Dumas, called the country of his birth 'The United Hates of America.' Pookie says it is a country where people 'save the whales, kiss the dogs, and slay black people just for a thrill.'"

Sherman stated, "Yeah, absolute truth." He went on to say, "There is a segment of the European community that just absolutely despises black people and hate us for no apparent reason. They have been convinced by the merchants. Those [merchants] are the people who are behind all this, the money-making people, the merchants; they have been convinced by the merchants that we are less than human. And because of that, they hate us."

A beat-around-the-bush type of person is not the way to describe Sherman L. Fowler. Directedness would be an accurate description of him. In *Islands of Thought, Pookie's Poetry*, Sherman eloquently describes a pathway leading to a location in Riam, Nigeria, that one cannot help but to feel as if they are there, seeing what Sherman poetically, simply describes, utilizing metaphors to place you there. I asked Sherman about this manner of speaking. I said to Sherman, "In the poem, 'On the Road Pass Riam, Nigeria,' you spoke of it with such admiration and beauty, and it helps to give you such a visual. I can feel nature down in my soul. This poem touched me in that way, but how did you come to be able to make words dance like that? They dance and they sing and they speak to one another in order to speak to you the reader. It's as Dr. Maya Angelou expressed, 'It's not something very public, and it's a personal thing when you write something like that. It comes from and speaks from your heart, not your mind. It's not as intellectual in that nature.' How do you come to write like that?" I asked.

Sherman had a very simple answer: "Well, I had great teachers, and one of them was the lady you just mentioned: Maya Angelou. She was a very close friend to my brother and mentor Eugene Redmond. We had her here (in Missouri) for a workshop back in the day. And I called her 'Auntie Maya.' She gave me some pointers and tips on writing, but I had already received a lot from Dumas and Eugene Redmond, but I had always expressed my thoughts, and when people would hear me read my poetry, they said, 'Man, you paint the picture. You've painted a picture!' I said, 'Well, I wasn't conscious of the fact that I was painting the picture. The way I see things, because I'm a photographer, I see pictures, and when I express myself, I paint pictures!"

I have only touched on a fraction of the people that have had an impact on Sherman's life, but I could not conclude the interview without an honorable mention of the late, great woman from Joliet, IL. An American dancer, choreographer, author, educator, anthropologist, and social activist, Katherine Dunham! I asked Sherman to talk about his experience with Katherine Dunham. He mentioned a lesson she taught him that struck me as one of the most profound lessons I learned during this interview, which by the way, amplifies the title and topic of Sherman's book he was interviewed for: thoughts!

"Katherine Dunham was the lady who made me understand that, you know, we tend to try to lump everybody into our way of doing things or our way of thinking. And I try; I learned from her that you don't try to get other people to think what you think. You try to get them to think! Get them to think; they may conclude what you conclude, but you have to get them there. Our people have been conditioned to follow and not think. We accept what people tell us…. It's trickled-down thought. Oh, they got the trickled-down economics, where the money is supposed to trickle down to the bottom and it never gets there. Well, trickled-down thought is the same way. Actually, every human being is an island of thought. We live in a universe of thoughts, and we are islands of thoughts, and we must, if we are to succeed, if we are to survive, we must begin to think and not accept what the authority is telling us. We've got to think for ourselves."

Before we end the interview, I want to address a couple of the other poems that Sherman just paints such a beautiful picture of having to do with the Million Man March of October 16, 1995, and the love of his life … his wife. This is what Sherman told me:

"It was the most spiritual experience I've had on this continent. I've had a lot of spiritual experiences in Africa, but that one was the most spiritual experience with black people that I've had on this continent. It was just purely spiritual. Juble Harrison, one of my protégés, captured the essence of that day in the poster that is paired with the book *Visible Glory*. On that day, there was no argument, no fighting; nobody was smoking dope. Nobody was drinking liquor. It was just a spiritual experience. Over a million black men concentrated in one place for one single purpose. We came to show them [government] that we could have a million men. We could marshal that many men!"

Finally, I asked Sherman to tell me about Peaches, his wife. "We were together for forty-nine years before she passed away. Just before she passed away, six months, she was ill at the time, and I think she knew she was getting ready to check out…. She told me, and these words resonate with me all the time when I think about her, she said that I was the best thing that ever happened to her, because her first husband ill-treated her and all I did was love her from the first beginning. I loved her, and I loved her all … all her life. When she was ill, I took care of her. My kids didn't help us … our kids didn't help us. It was just me, and I had a heart attack taking care of her. That's how much I loved her."

One of my biggest take-a-ways from this interview is that Sherman L. Fowler, AKA "Pookie," does everything with passion. He speaks with poetic passion, his photography shows his visual passion, and he loved his wife with unconditional passion! In a world full of anger and even rage these days, the poetic passion of Sherman L. Fowler is a welcomed reprieve, and I relish in the island of my thoughts imagining that his next work of poetic art, *Facets of Life*, will put a brilliant shine upon one's soul!

When Sherman was born, his parents, David Otis and Easter Mary Fowler, lived in East St. Louis, Illinois. He was born in St. Louis, Missouri, because St. Mary's hospital in his parents' hometown did not allow black children to be born in that hospital. He grew up in East St. Louis, Illinois, and attended the same elementary school his mother had attended with Miles Dewey Davis. Sherman was fortunate to have been instructed by a relative of Nat Turner—Lucy Turner—at Crispus Attucks elementary.

He also had the great fortune to accompany his father to places his father frequented and to meet some of his dad's friends, like Miles

Davis, Leo Gooden, Eugene Haynes, and other hip people finding their way in an America that was their home, like it or not.

On many occasions, with his dad, they would attend some of the local bars and twelve-year-old Sherman was allowed to sit at the bar next to his dad. He recalls being like a sponge and would take in all that was being discussed about race relations, politics, who had the best weed, etc.

Facets of life is an inciteful and inspirational poetic drink—straight no chaser (a request he often heard at the Sportsman Lounge when patrons would order their drinks). He queried his father as to the meaning, and came to understand it meant an undiluted drink, and the next time he sat at the bar and the bartender asked what he wanted, he replied, "Coke—straight no chaser" (a phrase that later became the title of a great jazz tune).

Sherman heard words and loved how they danced in his young mind, inspiring him to develop a notebook and write the words and pictures the universe bestowed upon his awakening consciousness.

The words in this book that play you a tune and paint you scenic views are facets of his life and the life of many others—spirits known and unknown.

S L A V E — L U N A C Y :
P R I S O N E R S   W I T H   J O B S

*(For my ancestors whose only crime was being dark-skinned
and vulnerable)*

       LOVE of money drove Europe's unscrupulous human
traders to
       CAPTURE unsuspecting, civilized, highly skilled, enlight-
ened African
People living harmoniously with their God-given culture
and independence
NOWHERE TO RUN—NOWHERE TO HIDE

Chained and bound, ferried like cargo to ports of commerce,
       Auctioned like cattle and sold as "SLAVES" to
greedy gullible
Buyers intent on owning unpaid captive LABORERS
NOWHERE TO RUN—NOWHERE TO HIDE

Named, claimed, still in chains, newly christened captives

       Were dispersed to plantation-prisons controlled by dupes

       With bogus receipts of CHATTEL ownership
NOWHERE TO RUN—NOWHERE TO HIDE

Under lock and key by night, forced to labor under the LASH
       By day overseen by two and four-legged guard dogs
trained to
Hunt and kill RUNAWAYS
NOWHERE TO RUN—NOWHERE TO HIDE

       Along came HARRIET with a train bound for FREEDOM
KNEW WHERE TO RUN—KNEW WHERE TO HIDE

HIS-STORY BOOK called it a "SLAVE TRADE"—
       Don't swallow the LYE
Any person that could conceive or believe a HUMAN
could BUY/SELL
       Or LEGALLY OWN another HUMAN had to be and
should have been
Declared LEGALLY INSANE

NOWHERE TO RUN—NOWHERE TO HIDE
    Is IMPRISONMENT not OWNERSHIP and being dark-skinned is not a crime
In the everywhere kingdom of a CREATOR
    Whose life, love, and liberty are for one and ALL
FREE BY GOD'S DECREE

MONEY TREE

Golden eggs are a trifle
If you possess the source
That lays golden eggs—
 Seek the SOURCE-IN-SOUL

IMPEACHMENT-2019

It was a dance
Of Republican dunderheads
Stomping and kicking to
Trumpety-tunes—
 Round by five-minute round—raising
Word-clouds to hide TRUTH
From THINKING eyes and ears.

SENTIENCE AND SAPIENCE

Two men walking.
Two men talking:
"We are because God is—
Whatever God is, we are."

"So isn't that the same
As I and my father are one?"
"Different words, same thought,
Same inevitable truth."

"So, we get to think on
This for an eternity?"
"Yeah."

"But what about the sleepers?"
"They will awaken in God's time."

CASH AND CARRY

Each holiday is a
    Pick your
Pocket day
Made to order
    For
Sleep-walkers—
A merchant's DELIGHT!

HEAVEN OR HELL

(For those who wish to know whether someone has been there or not.)

In the boxing ring of life,
THINK for yourself at all times.
Beware! Holy hypocrites preach what they don't practice,
Practice what they won't preach—teach what they don't know,

Won't teach what they do know—will tell you of places they
Haven't been, cannot tell you of any person that has been
To the places they haven't been, and returned to school us!

Beware! Holy hypocrites will sell you an empty glass of water
TO QUENCH YOUR THIRST.

HOT-AIR RIDE

En route from Paris, leisurely floating
Over sun-soaked Sahara sands
Jet-bound for Lagos we were
Gently rocked from side to side

Like a baby in a cradle by hot
Desert up-draughts, while
 Embracing lingering visions of Italy's
Boot in the blue Mediterranean Sea
We crossed earlier.

SAY WHAT?

Let me get this straight—you are sincerely
Telling me I should absolutely
         BELIEVE/ACCEPT

As TRUTH that a man who couldn't
READ OR WRITE

Traveled about speaking to multitudes who
Couldn't

READ OR WRITE, was murdered by people who couldn't
READ OR WRITE, and

After he had been dead for over a thousand years,
His verbatim words and speeches were enshrined

In the first ever Bible/Book compiled by a man who could
READ AND WRITE … SAY WHAT?

FLIGHT TIME

On an overnighter from O'Hare international,
Chi-town,
We were awakened by the captain, greeted
With a hot towel to the face as we descended
From 35,000 ft. to put feet down at Schipol
International, A-dam.

AT THE CLUB

On the dance floor, she was
     Movin' and groovin' in a
PEEK AT YOU mini-skirt
       Buttocks busier than a
Worm in hot ashes.

ONE
LIKE beauty, love is ubiquitous
      And
All humanity is blood-linked
      And
Soul-bound.

A TIGER'S TALE

(For my friend Jumane Lowery)

Lincoln's magician could
      Make a football disappear
On a quarterback boot-leg
      Touch-down run; learned to
Make heroin disappear up
      His arm—overdose made him disappear
Later in life.

SOUTHERN DISCOMFORT-1960

(For Sam Cooke, who predicted a change would come)

On leave from Fort Jackson, South Carolina,
Homeward bound on a Greyhound—
A food stop in rural Georgia some thought
Was a fool stop

White folk could enter and wait to be served
Niggers could go round yonder and buy
They sandwich at the back door

Five dark faces dressed in U.S. Army green
Money-in-pocket, no food in hand
Back on bus, belly on back wouldn't

Eat until St. Loo, hunger was the
Least of their pains—they pondered if a fool
Could ever change and if the America

They had been prepped to fight for would
ALWAYS REMAIN THE SAME?

OWL TALK

Life, it is what it is,
You can make of it
What you will—
If you will.

A SOFT WET KISS

(For fond memories of Plateau State, Nigeria)

A shape-shifting cloud
    Entered our high-rise flat
Tiptoeing through an open
    Bedroom window to hug-kiss
My wife and I, lingering until
    It was touched by the evaporating
Embrace of sun—blanketing
    Mile-high peaks in Jos.

A POET'S DESIRE

Happiness is contagious;
    May all who encounter it
Be infected by its
transformative power.

UNKNOWN—NEVER KNOWN

Life is a revolving door
    Life comes, life goes—
From whence life comes
    And where life goes
No person knows
    Life is a mystery known only
To the creator of Life's
    Ever-revolving door.

RAP-WRITE

Lift your kin-kind
From the quicksand
Of untruth, awaken

Them with clarity of
Thought—rapped or penned

Never leave them mired
In the mud of confusing
Mysterious misunderstanding

Heads aren't meant to
See the world while

Standing on them—
Treat don't trick

KWANSABA UJAMAA: PATHWAYS

There are no easy paths in the
Forest that lead to the sea of
Free; people united make new trails for
Their beloved kin and kind. Push and
Pull, give and take, people create what
Is desired in accord with what they
Discern is best for one and all.

NO TRIPPING

Mary Jane will lead
You to the HIGH in
Your mind; when
You fathom that HIGH
Is a state of mind, you
Will no longer court
Mary Jane to get high.

BIRDS

Unlike caged birds, caged people
Don't sing, they discern it is arduous
To swim upstream—realize
Living in a cage
 Is a nightmare no person
Should dream.

ELEMENTS

Rain clouds ride wind-horses;
Rain can't go where
 wind won't
Take it; some places never see
Rain's face—nor kiss her sweet
Wet lips.

SALVATION

Said the self-appointed saint
To the sinner-designate:

"Join the Church; accept Christ.
You will be saved and dwell
In the kingdom of God forever."

Said the sinner-designate
To the self-appointed saint:

"Saved from what? For what? I
Have always been a permanent
resident of God's kingdom—you

Should know that when God
Was we were, or we wouldn't be."

COKE

Far too many
    Snort dust,
Became dust
      Far too soon.

WITHIN—WITHOUT

Things are not wealth,
Their lack not poverty;
Wealth is abundance inherent within;
Poverty is an illusion of being
Without—a child of ignorance.

THIEVES OF D.C.

(For Michael Castro 1945-2018)

Truth, an insult to a fool,
Wisdom tells us broke-brained people prefer
Shadow to substance, fantasy to reality

Skin color to character, ignorance to knowledge,
Deceit to honesty, blindness to vision,
Evil to good, war to peace

Hate to love, nonsense to sense,
Lies to truth—hawked to you
By White House soul-twisters.

ILLUSIONS

Dreamed on dope—pissed on hope
Didn't wanna cope—didn't wanna scope
No more poor Joe.

Swung low in the ghetto
Dealing death to soul-bloods
In alleyways of the hood.

Song of siren wailed a sad lament—
Joe was gunned down, another
Dope-hawkers life's been spent.

EYES IN THE BACK OF THEIR HEADS

(For the victims of crack)

Bones snake through the gizzard
Of the city—cracked in search of
Vaporous illusions to dine on

In search of vaporous illusions
To ride on—in search of vaporous
Illusions to die on.

JUJU MAN

Dream spinner eyeing
Yet-to-be sunrises—soul
Immersed in potent
Thought—with your
 God-self.

UNIVERSAL GLUE

Love's power incomprehensible to
Gun lords force barons murder masters
Grave burglars land lifters people procurers
Atomic terrorists cross-burning hooded
Night stalkers—Love's antithesis.

DREAM MACHINE

(For all who use their head for more than a hat rack)

Clouds parade across sky's face
Stars wink at lovers—gazers who
Drink wind's sweet-milk and
Dream

Take time to dream—take time to love
Love gives birth to love in cycles of
Never-ending love and dreams are

Pathways to isles of adventure,
Vaults of untold riches, blueprints
For success, gateways to freedom—

Doors to health and happiness:
Dream and love the dream.

THAT LADY

Her smile makes sunshine brighter
Clouds glow whiter—life's burdens
Lighter; a grateful soul rejoices at
The touch of her eyes—surrenders
to her captivating charm.

LIFE-WAYS

There was a time before time
There were no stars to shine
Life lived and had its being
In an indivisible eternal soul-self
Life begat time, there are
Stars to shine—life lives,
Moves, has its being in
An indivisible eternal soul-self
That walks and talks—
What was, is—what is
Keeps on groovin'.

THE ELECTRIC EYES OF
OCTOBER: 1995

Electric eyes witness:
One million Black heads
Lashed tight, harmonious in
Mystical concentration—
Power to invert a down-presser
Nation.

Electric eyes witness:
One million Black heads
Focusing self on self,
Power to kick-start a
Sleeping giant—possess
A universe.

LAMENT FOR JESSE

Braked at a stop sign
Passing through wheeler-dealers' row,
Eyes focused on a figure, a childhood
Pal rushing to get his lush on.

Intent on cooking his head,
Oiling his super-thin body with
The current cash-and-carry eye blinder.

His sad eyes spoke of a broken love-nest
And he swims in a blue grape sea

Drowning daily—murdering infinite
Potential for greatness.

MARRIAGE

His soul was owned by the
Woman he wed—
His body performed in
Many women's
Bed.

HEY LADY LOVE: FOR SHIRLEY BRADLEY LE FLORE

Your inherent beauty and
Wit
Radiates from your majestic smile
Like a newborn
Sun—strolling
Across the Ethiopian sea.

MISGUIDED

Folly dozes in the head
Of the ignorant—
Awakens in the hammock
Of hate.

BIRDY BYE

Night covers my house
Silence prowls in
My room until
Miles enters my body
On a wave of soft
Sensuous East St. Louis coolness
 That massages my soul—
I fly swiftly to a sea of dreams
And bid bye to a trumpeting bird in black

KITIMBO/MAKIN' WHOOPEE

Intertwined in copulation
Man and woman
Kitimbo ... Movin'
To vibes only they can hear—
Doing the dance of love.

DUNHAM'S DANCERS:
FOND MEMORIES
The holy hands of Haiti's master
Drummer, Rene' Calvin,
Spanked goat booty, invoking
Spirits in bodies
To Yanvalou for you.

Enchanting, statuesque figures moved
Across the stage
Like a hungry serpent in
The bush
Stalking a meal to kill—
Dambala has come to give
Us a thrill.

DEXTING: FOR DEXTER
GORDON 1923-1990
Dexting a melody
That stepped out of a
Dream, after having
A swinging affair with
Le Coiffeur,
Who moaned and groaned like
A trilling tenor sax
Climaxing round midnight—
What is this thing called love?

Darn that dream dropped
Harmonious love-bombs,
Raining sonic-solace
On a soul that knows it can
Never die—
As time goes by, please forward
This Dext to all
Yo' peeps.
C.C.:
Dr. Red

GENESIS

THOUGHT gave rise
To a UNIVERSE—
Capture the rapture of that
Immeasurable entity
Evolving in the matrix
Of SOUL—the
Essence of all life,
All being,
All things.

MIRED MINDS

Racist stew in a putrid cesspool
Of ignorance and infectious
Hatred; they
Desire to obtain an unobtainable
Pure blood-line
And spread their foul, diseased doctrine
That falsely proclaims a superior
Human race.

SHE: FOR BILLY HOLIDAY 1915-1959

Beauty radiates from adorable
Sage-brown eyes like a naked
Starlet prancing
Amongst stars on a night
When a musical genius birthed—
"God bless the child that's got his own."

SEEKERS
Let God be your
Only guru;
You will pay nothing,
Gain all—
Only God knows
The will of
God.

SWEET AND SOUR
Miles Davis gave us
Sketches of Spain;
Old age gives us
Sketches of pain—
Melodies and maladies
Of life.

MUD IN YOUR EYE
Know-it-all charlatans
Blind people with tales of a story-book
Deity,
Leaving them groping in darkness
Unable to discern
The light of the omnipotent
Deity within,
The deity without,
The deity that's all in all—
The deity that's all about.

TRANE RIDE
Miles took a trip
On a Trane and
He thought about you—
So what?

FOREVER PREGNANT
Now and always are
Twins
In the eternal womb
Of soul
Where all life and things
Await their time to be
Born.

MAN-MADE REALITY
An addiction to the words of
Pious men
Imprisons believers, wrapping them
In a cloak of ignorance, compelling
Them to see
Life through the eyes of
Pious-pretenders.

UNBOUND
Rise from the bonds of
Ignorance,
Be reborn in the savvy-glow
Of wisdom, knowledge, and understanding—
Catch a horse named desire; ride till
You die.

A BALL OF CONFUSION: 2019

In that senate-impeachment farce, reason
Was out of season,
Sanity failed, executive lawlessness prevailed
Putting democracy in the I.C.U. and it's
Not doing well—suffering from
A lack-of-brains disease

Will somebody please ring the justice bell
And send that wig-wearing Lysol-hawker,
 Misfit-dunderhead-senator
 And the rest
Of Russia's U.S. crazy goons to a prison with
Windowless cells—
America, wouldn't that be swell?

If you like it, shatter silence
With a thunderous yell—
At the polls—2020.

COLD HEADS

Hatred is a beast
Kept frozen
In the ice of stupidity
To keep it
From knowing the joys and
Warmth of love.

SLEEP STATION

My friend sleeps
In a mask; I am told
It is not to hide her face.
It is to keep her face
In the valley of the living.

RELATIONSHIPS

Sexual attraction is a trap
Love has devised
To ensnare humans—bind
Them for eternity.

HAIRSTYLES

The do on your
Head is not
As important as the
Do in your head.

CAPTIVITY

Before men bound other
Men
Men bound dogs to perfect
The art of
Dependence and control
Of
Body and soul.

RISING-RIVER BLUES: FLOOD OF '93 IN ST. LOUIS, FOR PAMELA A. ESCARCEGA

Got the river blues, water rising, rising,
Rising, giving us those rising-
River blues
Have you heard the news? Many
Farmlands drowned, homes are empty
Yachts and moneymaking is on
Forced vacation—sho'nuff
Suffering, suffering from those
Rising-river blues.

Old muddy river doesn't care 'bout
No new homes,
Don't know right from wrong.
River just do what river naturally do—
Impregnating flood plains, causing
River dwellers pain and
Suffering-blue.
Old muddy river never knew
River just do what river naturally do.

Got the rising-river blues
Water rising, rising, rising,
Giving us those rising-river blues.
Haven't you heard the news?
Rising river has given us blues
And more blues; we seek
Spirits counsel to experience
Spirit's good—listen to the news,
So much water, God put on his overshoes.
We pray, we love, we care, no more
Blues; no more blues—no more
Rising-river blues.

CHARLES GARDEN RETIREMENT COMPLEX: COVID-CRISIS 2020

(For Joyce and Diane)

At a happy hour record spin, "Smokey" was crooning
"Shop Around."
Worldwide, Coronavirus was doing the
Hop around;
Residents are on lock-down, home-bound, to
Avoid being laid to eternal rest—
In the ground.

LESSON #222

In the enchanted embrace
 Of night,
When stars are
All aglow, you can hear
Silence roar—talk to God,
God will talk to you, in your
Solitude.

LESSON # 255

Mistakes are the sun, rain,
And fertilizer essential to grow
Wisdom, knowledge, and understanding
In the sacred garden
Known as life.

MACKIN'

Man said to woman,
"They have machines for this
And machines for that; I am
A baby-making machine—
Plug me in."

ROOTS

Love's roots are divine;
Hate's roots thrive in an
Ignorant mind.

AUTOMATIC SYSTEMATIC MIND-BANG

Media-made reality is as perfect as
It gets in grinding
Humans into rubbish, making them
Coins of the same kind
With one robotic upside-down mind.
You dare not think free, freely think,
Or have any thoughts not made by
TV.
People worship media without regret,
Are mind-banged till they forget
That they are life's drumbeat—
Not slavish sheep to grovel at a media-
master's feet.

IN THE NAME OF A GOD
WITH NO NAME

Stealth fighters in the still of the night
Let fly ravenous beasts of destruction
We see on TV the blasting of God's own
By smart bombs vaporizing people and property—American
 Armed forces attack Iraq.

Four-legged beasts are given more respect
Than government's public-enemy number one—
Let fly weapons of mass destruction to destroy
Weapons of mass destruction, and of course,
Kill Saddam and Co.

Let us forget that war begets war
Not peace, but bits and pieces of
Dead people scattered in rubble and debris
Never to resurrect.

Let us kill, kill, kill till we reach that hill
Where God lives and let us kill again—
By the way, it will be televised.

AFRICAN ASSIMILATION

America raised its dark-lovely step-children
Of the stars
And stripes in its own euro-centric image,
Taught them French songs, German dances,
English profanity
Christian beliefs and alcoholic stupefication—
Leaving them void of self-knowledge.

Taught them to steal and
Preached to them
Not to steal, while she conspired to steal their soul.
Taught them dependence, how to say, "Massah"
How to hate themselves; love others—now
Ain't that mucked-up?

Advocated melting-pot theories,
Hero-heroine-heroin worship—how to
Snort coke and blow smoke in the
Face of God.
Promoted religious rituals that infested
Their souls
So that they thought in confusion and
Knew not their ancestors' wisdom.

Scanning her own euro-centric image in the
Mirror of their
Attitudes, America saw her own ugly ways
Reflected in black-face and hated them
All the more.

They climbed the mountain of self-consciousness,
Found self-love, self-reliance, sagacious-self
Development and African-reflection.
A reverence for African-cultural intercourse, romancing
Their own God-given inheritance—having love and
Respect for the universe they share with all.

Truly free, they see through their own spirit-eyes
Ascending to soar prolific, quench their thirst
From the infinite
Well of their ancestral-essence-self and
Dream-weave their own afro-centric realities.

LOVELY AS A POEM

Buried, rooted
Sunk solidly in earth,
Immobile,
You spring-rise
Shoot skyward
Multiple arms branching
From a bark-encrusted body.

Searching fingers
Budding green
Kiss sun
And
Finger-coitus wind.
In cycles and circles
You change again and again
And again—
Come spring, you
Clothe winter nudity
Giving refuge to homeless wings.

TRADIN' TIMES

In the shadow of a cross
Honey-hawkers slut-strut a city street
Lean in windows
Make deals for thrills with Johns
On wheels

$50 will get you everything
From AIDS to zeds
Around the world and back again
How about it, friend?

Can I get in,
Spit-shine your Johnson
 While we take a spin
Around the world and back again?

How about it, friend?
Around the world and back again?
Come on, baby, let's take that spin.
$50 will get you everything.

AN ENCOUNTER ON THE SAVANNAH

The first time
I came face to bark
With a Baobab
On the Nigerian savannah,
I was in awe of its majesty.

It has a strange sort
Of beauty and is an
Excellent teacher,
Teaching me that God
Has a joyous sense of humor—
Only God could conceive
An upside-down tree.

SUMMER LOVE

(FOR HARMONICA DON HOFFMAN)

There's nothing better
Than a
Home-grown just-picked
Tomato that has been
Kissed by summer sun
And romanced by the
Elements

GREATEST POUND FOR POUND: # 50

On that historic night
In Vegas
A hunter chased his prey
Trapped him and knocked
Him out
He pulled his bodacious tongue
From swollen lips
And wrote: "You can't beat me"
On his freshly skinned hide.
"I am Floyd 'Money' Mayweather"

TRUTH BE TOLD

Family and friends are friends
Indeed, whose hands
Are held out when in need, but
Don't ask them to return or lend a hand;
They will vanish faster than mornin' dew
At sunrise on the
Western edge of the Kalahari where
The Atlantic has
Intercourse with the world's oldest known desert.

FIRES BY THE ROAD IN KADUNA, NIGERIA

In the flames of the fire burning
The wood that's warming
Us from cold desert winds
Ghostly
Shadows lounge in flickering
Flames roasting sweet Suya meat
Where the scent of ginger lingers
Flames that spark wonder in
The soul we call self—
Blazing life-trails that illuminate truth
And burn no flesh

BAR BEACH

Restless waves are assaulting
The sandy beach, nibbling its
 Flesh
A man stands alone in knee-deep water
Rocked by waves and rising tides
Transfixed by an image eyeballing
A crescent moon in a star-flecked sky

In awe, he joins the multitudes of witnesses
Before him and offers his silent
Desires to the Maker—mounts
His horse, rides along the
Moonlit beach, and becomes
One with the Lagos night

JOS PLATEAU, NIGERIA

A man sat amongst the rocks
Listening to a tale of wind—
Wind whispered to him how she
Was first formed in the mouth
 Of God
God spat her out to set
The earth spinning, forming night
And day
Weather and seasons
Wind has to always move while
She shapes earth's face, making
High and low places so she
Can speak to men who listen

ABEOKUTA, NIGERIA:
KINGDOM OF JUJU MEN

In the village of Lapaliki, I become one
 With magic
Juju and I marry beneath
Palm trees shading a stream-fed
Pool where village men bathe
An old woman walks an ancient
Trail, which passes the pool
On her head she carries a load of
Firewood
She sees me standing in the pool in
My nudity and I vanish before
 her eyes
She passes and I am transported to days
Of yore when kidnapped men, women, and
Children were dragged in chains
Kicking and screaming, ferried to a world
Not of their making—
They had not learned the magic of
Becoming invisible

LOVE THYSELF—THYSELF LOVE

All must live in the
Web of love
Even though they may not
Meet in time and space
Love is a refuge—always an
Essential tree of life
Flesh and blood must rot
And dry
No reason to cry
 Love sustains soul's self—it's
imperishably
Ubiquitous

FRUIT FOR ONE AND ALL

Thrivin' within the vault of
Our soul-self
Copious thought cheerfully constructs
Poly-channels of supply

To bathe us in total joy
And bend the bough of
Our life's tree with
Abundant fruit

THE MIND AT WORK

Dare to be more than a chump
Locked tight in mental slavery
Think things
That go sailing in the sky
Flying without wings
Mind at work creates thought-things
Lightning flashes of ideas
Shock grey-matter thought-things
We see infinite in thought
We be and free
To think-dream our own
Reality
Dare to dream—dare to be
A dreamer of dreams, a creator
Of thought and things

LAGOS IN SPRING: A SEASON OF RAIN AND DREAMS

Old and young faces spanning earth's
Color spectrum of skin
Co-mingle in this house of temporary
Lodgers
Travelers, visitors, hustlers, and
Sightseers going up and down
Like rhythm
Rising from drum-skins—
A melody of human bubbles
Form a pool where no fish swim

Early risers encounter spring's fragrant
Aromas as they stroll past
High-rise dreams, casting their shadows
Over the city-scape
Home-grown thinkers, in the busy-ness
Of day, fashion new dreams

To replace old dreams—
Thought gives birth to thought
Mind energizes mind, spawning
 Visions of future-spring—
In spring when
Spring is breaking water

IDOLS

They hung Rome's home-made religion
Around our necks
Collared, we dangle addicted in the
Noose of a spell
Adrift on a river of ignorance anchored
To a cross
Too awed by the idol and bound
By fear to
Seek consciousness—find self in
The free-sea of mind
Unfettered

LONGINGS

Longing can find you day-dreaming
In windowless windows
Aloof at parties, dazed at work
Alone in crowds
Desiring, seeing, being all that
 You long for ...
Longing will have you watching
Leaves flutter,
Drunk on a jazzy tune—awoke
At midnight
Staring into the dark alone
Desiring, seeing, being all that
You long for
Longing is living, desiring, seeing, being—
All that you long for

SUNRISE-EAST

River valley, flood-plain swamp reclaimed
Matrimonial teepee
Of bloodlines old and new

Stockyards, Monsanto farts, smoke stacks
Railroad tracks
Barbequed snoots, Beckerman boots, a church
Here, a tavern there, a drunk everywhere,
Scholars aplenty I swear and artists
In the abode of the cool lash of the fool
And big-booty capital

Tigers, flyers, flying tigers, trolley cars, candy
Bars
Crawling trains, speedy brains, gambling dens
Life-long friends
Enjoy a roasted goat, a funky blue note
A jazzy jump, a big fine rump, an afternoon
Hump
 A funky stomp in East St. Louis'
Valley of soul—
Sunrise-east where kings and queens manifest dreams
By timeless muddy-'sippi-water

GUNLORDS

(For Ishaq Shafiq)

They performed larceny on our ancestral
Tongue to fashion
A slave-designate who could not speak
The music ancient as breath, so we would
Not recall words and deeds of Shango
 And Ogun
That should have been blown on us at
Cradle's edge
In Yoruba sing-song—so we would not traverse
Logic paths conjured by Olodumare
Whose thought-ways blossomed a get-down culture
Long before King James
And Co. replaced our father's heads with
Their father's heads—amputated our God-
Given mother tongue
Grafting English in our African mouths
Dumping English culture in our African-
stew, TRANSPLANTING
English indoctrination to eradicate African Juju—the sleeper
does arise
To RISE

TEARS FOR ADE—SEEDS OF HOPE

I weep for Ade; crocodile tears cascade down
My face
To splatter and become one with dust
Ade the dreamer who dared believe he could
Do great deeds
Could achieve new realities for self and kind
Mounted a steed called faith but could not
Endure to the fruiting
Season and for that reason he descended from
Grace to disgrace
To ride a Forty-Oz mule in circles of despair
I weep for all the Ades God loves, my tears
A sea of hope seeds to be
 Nourished by God and
explode to resurrect joy—
Manifest dreams

REFLECTIONS OF MAIDUGURI

(For Professor Akinsola Akiwowo who took me there)

Maiduguri of the rounded Mosque and chanting heads
Facing Mecca
Communing with Allah
Maiduguri of the brightly dressed Arabian equines
Ridden through paved
And unpaved streets by well-dressed dark-skinned
African thinker-men
Maiduguri of the hot desert breath and cold
Harmattan winds
Mosquito-netted nights in vice chancellor's guest quarters
University of Maiduguri
Where English indoctrination in African education
Did not take root
In a culture that produced scholars, artists before the
Intervention of English education
Maiduguri of the giant green fly and fly-infested
Meat-markets
And hot charcoal fires that cleanse and roast the
Meat delicacy Suya
Maiduguri of the crescent moon and star-faced nights
Creative imagination in flight
Think-dreaming a better reality for a world being
Born with new-think
Maiduguri of the Hausa tongue, of well-stocked
Markets
Gold, silver, and copper jewelry—leather, wood
And numerous artifacts
Fashioned by African minds and hands
Maiduguri of past, present, and future African culture—
Maiduguri of Akinsola Akiwowo's Nigeria

PORTRAIT OF A SEX FIEND

(A brainstorm by Eugene B. Redmond and Sherman L. Fowler
on the way to the airport}

His brain fell
Between his legs
And he was out of it

MY QUEEN

Brown forest flower
Love flower of the forest
Queen mother of men

A TONIC FOR THE SOUL:
THE BITTER TRUTH

(For Lori Reed, Ruby Smith & others of the diaspora)

Coerced labor of any kind is bad and were it not
For the acceptance of
A soft indulgent form of coercion on African soil
Maybe there wouldn't have been raids on sleeping
Villages—pillages of same
By African-dupes collaborating with European merchants
Maybe there wouldn't have been white-winged
Birds of the sea
Gliding—riding the waves, ferrying kidnapped Africans
A people once so free
Maybe there wouldn't have been Georgia plantation
Hands working under
The lash on ole master's land
Coerced labor of any kind is bad and were it not
For the acceptance of
A soft indulgent form of coercion on African soil
Where coercion of any kind should have been
A distasteful, wasteful use of the human
Body and mind—we
Would have been born AFREEKAN CITIZENS

BEFORE US

Before us, dreamers, seers, prophets shaped
Future-time before
Future-time became today-time
They bled, suffered, triumphed—crossed
Hot sands of life to find themselves at the
Cold waters of forced labor and the dirt road
Of lost freedom
Where love and hate collided at the red-light
Of plantation civilization
Be a hopeful dreamer, focus on truth,
Hang and hold
Be bold dreamers; set the goal
Hang and hold

Before us, ancestral engineers constructed faith
Bridges to leap
Chasms of doubt and despair—wove a rope
Of love connecting us to our source, our 911
Be a hopeful dreamer, focus on truth,
Hang and hold
Be bold dreamers; set the goal
Hang and hold
Before us—delivered us to achieve the goal

LADIES OF THE LIGHT-FEET

(For the dancers of the world)

Feet-light ladies of the light-feet
Dazzling
Stage romancers
Image enhancers
Glide like rainbow-colored auroras

Feet-light ladies of the light-feet
Electric
Twirling within shimmering beams
Stepping
Stradling
Swirling
Shaking
Whirling
Compelling

Muscles to move and groove with alacrity
Perform wonderous locomotion
In tempo and tandem with tone and bone

Feet-light ladies of the light-feet
Floating like Springboks on the African savannah
Getting down on ethereal
LIGHT-FEET

WITCHES' TRICKS

Sometimes in life false dreams are cast
In children's minds
Dreams arising from drug-induced
Vaporous illusions—while true realities lie like
Old discarded books
Collecting dust in dark non-inhabited
Corners of mind
Watch out for witches' tricks
Watch out for lies they tell
Watch out for the soul-slashing skag they sell
Witches will lock your mind in a fool's cell

RELIANCE

Realize, trust the omnipotent spirit
That imagined self
To be human and generously and perpetually
Provides for self—
Satisfying all needs, desires and creates
Channels of choice to manifest abundance
For its human existence.

GOOD LOVIN' MAMA BLUES

I know my baby love me
Cause she treats me
Oh, so good

I know my baby love me
Cause she treats me
Oh, so good

She gives me plenty lovin'
Just like a good woman should

She loves me in the mornin'
She loves me in the evenin'
Too

She loves me in the mornin'
She loves me in the evenin'
Too

And some fine day
She gonna make me say I do

I say some fine day
She gonna make me say I do

She's my good lovin' mama
She knows how to treat me good
She my good lovin' mama
She sure knows how to treat
This man good

She gives me plenty lovin'
Just like a good woman should

DR. SOUL
Soul doctors
Inject sage-speak
into the
Ignorant
And
Prejudiced—attempting
To cure hatred.

LESSON # 133
Become infected with love
Endless love
Get on up with love:
In the cities
In the country
On the highways and byways

Get on up with love
In the mornin'
In the afternoon
In the early night
In your midnight sleep
Love long and deep

Get on up with love
For the human race
With its many colors of face
And souls of grace—love and
Catch the boomerang

PROBE

Surely something as inconsequential as skin
Could never be a measure of men—
Could it?
Probe vital unapparent omni-present spiritual
Verity
To measure human-kin
Probe deeper, probe essence which manifests
As all manner of men-kin, in
 Various shades of skin.

FOREST SPIRITS

Dust rises in synchronized rhythm
With movement
Of feet responding to chants from
Goat-head drums and juju incantations
By forest spirits giving thanks to the
God-self for their being

GRANNYLOSOPHY: THINK AND GROW WISE

Granny said:
 "Mind is a wonderful source to
Explore.
Awake! Sons and daughters of
Eternity—
Glow with the soul-light of
Self-consciousness—manifest God's self:
YOURSELF.

"Within mind sublime, mine amazing
Realities
Born of soul-funk—sparks of divinity
Hatching
Soul power to sustain self, create
New truth, and
Like air, rise to the skies, to the stars and beyond."

SOUL-ROCK

Soul is the cornerstone upon which
We dream-build
Our bridges, spanning all chasms—
Be they made of doubt or despair,
Destitution or dissolution.

DRUM-TREES

In the forest of Nigeria there is wood
So hard
That if termites tried to bite it—
They would break their necks.

SOUL TO SOUL

In the closet of your sacred soul, be kind
To yourself—pay
Your daily respects to God with
Sincere humility and immeasurable
Gratitude

U.S. AIR-BASE: SPANGDAHLEM, GERMANY 1962

Black soldiers were not welcome in the
Village of Spangdahlem.
It was off-limits for Niggers to frequent
Whites-only bars or mayhem would ensue.
Blacks could travel miles to
Bitburg
To get their party on at bars that would
Accept U.S. dollars from
Dark-skinned military-men.

It was more than wine, women, or soul music
On the juke-box
That enticed them; it was the boiled
Pig feet and deep-fried Schnitzel that kept
Them coming back—they had a desire for the
Familiar and
An acquired taste for the new.

RENT A SLAVE: CASH MADAM

Pookie says:
"She wears her skirts thigh-high and
Stands on dimly
Lit corners flashing her goodies.
You can rent her for an hour, a day,
A month or longer.
If your cash stash is deep enough
She will be your lollipop on top, your joy
Or your toy.
She'll even be your full-time honey if you
Have the right amount of money.
She is always ready to please if you need
A temporary slave."

HOT FLASH

I am caressing her
Pressing my face against
Her slim black body...
My exploring finger touches
Her motion button, she
Exposes the object of
My fevered passion...
Best picture I've
Ever taken of a rose.

EYE CONTACT

Pookie said:
"The look in her eyes
Said it all:
'I am hot; please don't
Stop.
I need you to stroke me, stroke me,
Until I pop.'—
Imagine what happened.

A GAME CALLED BELIEVE

It is said that wise and erudite men and women,
Seekers of understanding and
Veritas,
Shun religious beliefs; they acknowledge
Religion as a creation
Of self-serving dubious
Men
Whose dupes pay a tax-tithe to be
Duped
With stories and doctrine that fly
From the mouths
Of those who cloak truth and knowledge
In mystery and myth.

Pookie says:
"Have the freedom of mind to think
For self, FATHOM
The CARROT and STICK game that dupers
Use to fleece
And control dupes;
Please don't condemn or declare a
Whistle-blower unholy, ungodly, or
Insane."

BEING THE GOAT: BE LIKE MIKE

M J understood that the tallest
Tree
In the forest is destined to be
Hunted by lumberjacks
With chainsaws,
Who are bound and determined to
Turn tall trees into fireplace
Wood—
Granny said: "Sometimes it is better to
Be seen and not heard."

BLOODLINES AND WATER CYCLES

A drop of blood from
Any person anywhere
Contains the blood of
All races everywhere
Like a drop of water from
Anywhere
Contains water from
Everywhere.
Can you dig it?

MEDIA AND THE PRESIDENTIAL PEEP-SHOW

It's sad.
Sad-sack sad.
Low-down dirty sad, even sad is sad.
My eyes are sad.
They have witnessed too many Lewinsky clips.
Too many Tripp clips.
Too many Starr clips.
Too many holier-than-thou clips.

The nation is sad; people worry about the economy,
Reporters are dispatched chasing tail-tales
About mouth-to-penis
Resuscitation—a two-year-old sperm-stained dress
And a twenty-two-year-old tattle-tale tell-all.
Media has become so blue-movie sad, so
Down-right peeping-Tom sad.

Maybe media will stop the sad massage, focus
People on stand-up
Solutions to world problems, catch some logic,
Exercise some sanity—
It's time to -30- the presidential peep-show,
It's so damn politically sad.

BUBBLE LIFE: WHAT WAS, IS

The air inhaled and exhaled
The water consumed and expelled
By animals and humans since the dawn
Of human and animal
Life has been recycled, passed on to
All breathers and waters drinkers
Living
On this spinning bubble called earth—
Continuously, yesterday, today, and for all
The days to come:
Same air, same water; no more, no less;
Shared by all life.

MUCHO CALIENTE

My friend Juan is quite the ladies man.
He enjoys
Many a one-night stand.
He met a hotty from Sri Lanka who
Called herself Harhenda;
She is the only woman to make
Juan surrender.
He found she enjoyed looking up
Much longer
Than he enjoyed looking down,
Causing him to say:
"No mas, baby, no mas"

FESTAC 1977—LAGOS, NIGERIA

Off-springs of mother Africa gathered in Lagos,
Native born and diasporic sons and
Daughters showed-up
To celebrate the Second World Festival of African Arts
And Culture.
World-renowned Chi-town jazz-genius Le Sun Ra was
A featured musician
Who packed the house beyond
Capacity.

The stage was set, lights up; sound
Erupted
To a thunderous applause that suddenly
Fell silent as
Ears and minds began to reel, attempting
To discern a melody
In the super up-tempo vibes bolting
Through the sound system.

Minds were drunk, confused by a chorus of buzzing
Bees and screaming
 Chainsaws—people panicked, fled the
Venue with alacrity; the few who stayed, endured
The hurricane and waited for
The tempo to slow, were blessed with
Le Sun Ra's melodious
Rendition of "My Favorite Things."

ELDORADO

I have found
Eldorado
Deep within myself
Abundance beyond measure
Deep within myself
I have found
Eldorado
In the abode of God
Deep within my soul's-self

IN THE MATRIX OF THE SOUL

Think about thought, peer into the
Infinite well from
Which it rises to grow—develop in
The matrix of
Imagination; manifest itself
As a poem, song, dance, or flying
Machine to proudly
Stand before us like majestic mountains
Dressed in Kente cloth.

FUNKING FOR ST. LOO

(For my friend and brother Quincy Troupe)

His tongue is a straight-back razor
Slicing and dicing
Words to be heard—projecting vivid
Scenes to be seen
In the theater of mind, featuring
Miles and Me.

DAVE'S MOOD: A GROOVE FOR DR. RED

All alone within a forest flower or sliding down
A trombone
To a Harlem nocturne, I love jazz on a foggy day
In London or an April in Paris
Blow me a mystery that will fly me to the
Moon or sweep
Me to the sunny side of the street where I can
Do a one-o'clock jump
Pat my feet to a Henry Dumas poetic beat and swallow a
Mood indigo of flutes—straight no chaser.

I cover the waterfront with daddy-Dave
Cause things ain't what they used to be
Somebody stole
My black and tan fantasy causing me to spend
A night in Tunisia—they can't take that away from me.
It's there I met Ruby and received a kiss to build
A dream on from Peaches: my woman
Of the world.
You can just sax me until I whistle, stars fell on Alabama
When it's sleepy time down south
Ballard me with Dex, that's my desire until I'm
Blue and sentimental
Then lose me in a rhapsody for a long, long
Summer

I'm in the mood for love, but I can't get started
Unless I hear
That Creole love call and somebody piano
Lady be good

Melody,
Jazz for me
Harmony,
Jazz for me
Melody,
Jazz for me
Harmony,
Jazz for me

Play me a riff like a runaway Trane on a track that leads
To sister Sadie's house
I need to keep body and soul together so I can Jody
Grind round midnight
At least once before the sorcerer bends me
An ill wind

Let me feel that thump thump thump of a bass
Come rain or
Come shine bewitching me with an autumn serenade
As I stroll
Among the pines taking giant steps near Dr. Red's
Place during the equinox and dare not go where fool's
Rush in
Fool that I am, I might give my foolish heart away on
A blue-moon night

I am truly a nightcrawler, living the street life so
Sweet and sour, greeting passing strangers on
The street where love lives
As I trumpet love songs dedicated to Sonny, Laura
And Naima too
Be careful when there's a moon over Miami—
Smoke gets in your eyes and that old black magic
Will bush-whack you; give you jive at five

Please don't talk about me when I'm gone, little darling
Cause sometimes I feel like sitting
On the dock of the bay daydreaming of faraway lands
Soon I'll be
Miles ahead of the game cause the creator has a master

Plan that is sure
To bring my ship laden with riches and gold
And I'll
Have this wonderful world on a string down
 Here on the
Ground and "Break Word" with
 My friend and mentor
Dr. Red.

LITTLE BIRD

In my youth I was lost
In a forest of
Misunderstanding; one day
A little bird landed on
My shoulder
And whispered in my ear:
"Bodies perish, souls are
Imperishable; you have a
Soul—be happy."
It flew away whistling
A tune
And I found myself in an orchard
Of ancestral understanding.

KEEPERS OF THE TORCH

We endured to strangle hoodwinking,
Brainwashing, sugarcoating and drove
A stake
In the heart of trepidation
We are keepers of a flame, branches on
An ancestor-tree
Walking on the waves of truth to stand
Vigilant—mind-locked on a vision of a black,
Brown and jazzy
Sunrise

ADEOLU AKINSANYA AND THE WESTERN TOPPERS

We enter the high-life club; it is dark and
We remain still
Until our eyes adjust, Baba Eto—the first
Father of music—
Is on the bandstand singing as drum rhymes
Bounce off walls and heads
Eko Angele he croons; the ladies of
Lagos move so saucy they appear to be
Angels walking on clouds

Apapa Jai, the albino guitarist, makes his high-life
Tuned guitar repeat the
Melody—Eko Angele, Eko Angele; Maria, Selena,
When I go see um!
The crowd explodes with laughter, their hands
Drumming applause
For the racy meaning of the words

Break-time and Baba Eto joins our table; we sip
Top beer, eat Suya
And he proposes a trip to his village in
Abeokuta
It is at the Olumo rock that our lives take a
New leap
We are propelled jet-like into the world
Of African spiritually
Where self finds self in the self of God

A MAN BY THE ROAD

On my way to the hidden village of enlightenment,
I encountered a man
Sitting by the side of the road, his face aglow with
Joy shining like
The noon-day sun—I enquired of him if he was the
Divine Holy one people say God sent to convert, assimilate,
And teach disciples; show them the way to the wonderful
And sacred abode of God

This he said to me:
"I do not claim to know the will of God,
I do not have a house of worship,
I do not convert, assimilate or teach disciples;
I offer no gospel or doctrine
Nor practice any religious rituals and
I only walk on water after sky has shed her joyful teardrops

"I know what I know cause I
Know—what I know—what I know I
Freely share
Cause the God I know, love, and immeasurably
Trust
Requires no tax-tithe to infinitely, abundantly, and
Constantly
Share all—with all

"Am I the Divine Holy one God has sent to convert, assimilate,
And teach disciples, show them the way to
The wonderful sacred
Abode of God, an everywhere place they already are
And always have been? Is this what people
THINK?"

FOR MAMA "D" AT 90

A jitterbug queen stepped into East Boogie's
Soul-scene
Star-dust-covered feet gracing legs adored by
World-eyes
Must be majesty in those thighs; Mama "D",
Katherine Dunham-elegant lady, Damballah's
Daughter
Whose serpentine movements have awed a
Generation of stars
Following that blazing comet's tail

Immortalized by Moguls of Hollywood, our
Sister of screen and stage was
Baptized by holy vibes of drum-voices—
She rides African
Rhythms to:
 Step and glide
Shake and slide
Twist and turn
Twirl and whirl
Like a dancing flower fresh from a
Haitian garden—
Inspiring aspiring dancers to blossom
And bear fruit

GOD'S WILL? REALLY

Pookie says,
"'GOD WILLS IT!'
Has been the rallying and motivational
Commandment
Of authoritarians, clerics, charlatans, despots,
And zealots
Since MEN created and organized
RELIGION
As a contrivance to acculturate, assimilate, convert,
Control and subjugate minds:
B.C. and A.D."

WILL I?

Logic compels me to know and
Understand
Above and beyond uncertainty and doubt
That eternal spirit
Will know and remember me
Eternally—Will I?
After my soul steps out of its
Temporary abode
To return from whence it came;
Will I know and remember me eternally?
Will I?

A NOTE FROM DR. SOUL

Haters' spoiled
Fruit produced
By the tree of
 Ignorance,
Kills give them thrills.

CHARLES "HANKY" CHILDRESS: 1937-2000

(A childhood friend)

In the early 1950s, people slept with
Their doors open,
Burned rags to chase mosquitos from
In houses and out-houses.
Charles lived with his cousin Lafayette
On 21st and Missouri Ave,
 East. St. Louis, Ill.

It was the radio era of Johnny Ace,
Howlin' Wolf, Nat King Cole, King
Pleasure, Billy Holiday, Count Basie,
Duke Ellington, and a young Miles
Dewey Davis who had not given birth
To the cool.

In my mind's movie, I can see Hanky, his
Long legs flashing
As he ran the football on the playground,
See him playing
Basketball and running track with his
Main man Preston Randolph.

Smooth, cool, and lanky, he had lots of
Friends: Jake Robinson,
Ozzie Fern, Julius Brown, Wilbur Meyers,
Curtis Thomas, Amos Leon Thomas, Roy
Mosley to name a few but not the many.

During the 1960s, the world spun war
And revolutions
Like smoke jumping out chimneys hurled
Into the wind.
No peace in the East, Viet Nam, Cuba, the
Congo
And in the streets of America.

After giving Uncle Sam his due, Hanky joined
The black revolution, hungry for a better
Life for black people.
Using his razor-sharp wit, he led—was
Always dapper in blue jeans, army boots,
And a black beret cocked
On the side of his afroed head; walking
Everywhere, and anywhere you found him,
He was preaching black pride.

He committed his life to black life, the
Revolution led him to Chicago with Lyon
Herbert, and Raymond Sharp, where they fought
A fierce gun-battle
With Chicago police—Herbert was killed,
Sharp and Hanky arrested and beaten
Senseless in Cook County jail to later
Be released without charges.

Hanky was never the same lightning-fast
Thinker he had been,
Never the same dedicated, determined
Human
He was destined to be…. Along with
Frank Childress, Eugene Redmond, James
Lewis, Raymond Sharp, Bennie Price,
Frank Bender and
A host of others, I raise my arm in
The black-power salute
To a fallen brother-warrior whose only
Crime was the love of his own kind—
Walk with God brother-man.

UNBALANCED

The grand lady JUSTICE is blindfolded,
She cannot
See crimes and atrocities committed
By the devious men
Who have blindfolded and control her;
Make rules for others
To OBEY and be weighed in the
UNBALANCED SCALES of INJUSTICE
She holds.

GRANNYLOSOPHY: TREASURES

Granny said:
"Know that health, joy, peace,
Love and freedom
Are treasures beyond measure
Contained in the vaults of body and soul—
This then is your WEALTH;
Money cannot purchase them; it
Can only
Assist you to enhance, maintain
And enjoy them."

GRANNYLOSOPHY: SHARING

Granny said:
"Refrain from hitting a fool over
His head
With truth, cause you could render
Him completely
Unconscious; instead, place truth in
His path so that he may stumble over
It and discover it for himself:

"You can lead a horse to water but
You can't make
It drink unless you force it and then
You might drown
The horse and spoil the water with
A dead carcass."

GRANNYLOSOPHY: STEP BY STEP

Granny said:
"All habits can be
Broken
If you desire and
Try—and really
Want to."

GRANNYLOSOPHY: BOYS WILL BE BOYS

(For a Man named George Floyd)

Granny said:
"Pity the foolish boys, boys who
Think because
They made killing humans an art
That gives
Them pleasure and joy they
Rule God's world
Which only good-old-boys should enjoy.
Pity those foolish immature
Little boys, those ignorant, deceitful boys
Dressed in BLUE
Hating on you who require malice, mayhem
And murder
To give them pleasure and joy.
Pity those little boys turning flips on a well-
Honed razor's edge—held in God's hand."

BEFORE YOU: FOR MY FRIEND AND FOREVER LOVE, HARRIETTE B.

Whenever I hear the lyrics of the song
"Before You," crooned by the
Duet of Sarah Vaughn and Joe Williams,
I am reminded
Of that fateful sunny day in May we
Locked eyes in 1967
On a sidewalk in East St. Louis, IL,
Where I handed you my heart and soul
To keep...
Until God sleeps; to never wake again.

RONA ON THE LOOSE: BEWARE

In my hood we don't wear mask
To look like
The Lone ranger or hide from a
Lone stranger—
We wear our mask to protect
Self from a human-hopping
Danger ... on the loose.

WHY DO THEY HATE US?

(For those who dance with ignorance and malice)

It is impossible to justify to
Yourself or to others
Why you would rape, rob, maim
Murder and subjugate people
You LOVE—
But you can LOVE to HATE
People not like you,
Allowing you to commit
Crimes and atrocities
Against them.

JOY

Rivers of joy
Flow
From waters eternal
Depositing
Life-giving fertility
Upon
Dry shores of souls;
Nourishing
Mankind—renewing self.

LESSON #322

Taste joy
Consume happiness
Embrace faith
Welcome wisdom
Abide in serene truth—
Fellowship with your divine self.

STRANDS

A spider's web
Of soul we are,
Each perfect strand
Woven together
Creating an indivisibly
Linked and
Connected universe of sentient,
Eternal, omnipotent,
Life and being.

HENRY LEE DUMAS: 1934-1968

(My brother and mentor)

The great God Shango
Crowned his head
With an endless sky
Of blue
Put unconditional love
In his soul ... he flew.

EUGENE HAYNES: 1927-2007
KWANSABA FOR AN EAST ST. LOUIS MAESTRO (An eternal friend)

An eagle began to spread wings wide,
Lincoln's budding genius touched ivory keys
Fingers notes that far exceed his grasp;
Boy wonder caught in the act playing
Stirs hearts, minds, soars swiftly to Julliard;
Miles joins him—they play fame game...
Hail Eugene Haynes high-soaring music maestro.

EDDIE FISHER: 1943-2007
SIPPIN' WITH THE FISH

(Great friend and brother)

Pour me a cup of music
Spiked with
Jazz; blues been bleached
Except in
Maude's flat.
Gonna' sip it nice
And slow
Painting the walls of
My soul
Grant Green and let my
Troubles go.

I like idle moments so I
Can contemplate....
What's going down?
What's going on?
What's going round?

I love that SOUND; those
Torrential waves haunt, taunt
Pursue me
Assaulting my eardrums, jazzy
Mysteries touching,
Swinging, ringing, singing to my head
Drowned in rhythms
Streaming from a stringed box.

Bonding, bounding, bouncing
Harmonies
Tease my imagination rendering
Me drunk, sedated—
Enraptured in a melody ... with
Funk flying joyously free
To kiss rainbows
And dance with moonbeams as

I do my THIRD CUP sippin',
Sippin', sippin with
The Fish-man—mellow as I
Can be:

I got it good and that
Ain't bad
I got joy and that
Ain't sad—pour me
Another cup, brother-man.

VET TALK: WHO WANTS WAR?

War is the worst thing
Humans created—
If you can go to war
To fight
And protect your country,
You should not
Hesitate to go to war and
Fight to protect
Yourself or your family.

HORIZONS: ABOVE AND BELOW

Wise—we rise
From the dust to
The skies, to
The stars and
Beyond
In dream ships
We pilot.

FOR MY BROTHERS
WEARING THE CROSS

Lest you forget:
It was the good Bible-toting
Scripture-quoting
Christian men and women who
Danced around that Godly-tree
Cheering and jeering at a
Cross-wearing innocent
Nigger they had just
Hung and gleefully set his
Body on fire—they were
Having-A-Party in Jesus' name.

AMOS LEON THOMAS: 1937-1999
JAZZ ME, BABY ... JAZZ ME ALL LIFE LONG

(My brother from another mother)

A soulful moaning from the belly of a
Saxophone,
Belly
Of a slave ship crossing over,
Belly
Of a woman giving birth,
Belly
Of a man making mirth.

Pick-pick-picking, picking
Cotton,
Picking strings, picking hideouts on the
Underground railroad,
Picking chitlins, picking greens, picking
Lovers, picking friends;
Picking life from the mind of God.
Wes thumps and bumps over city
Sounds:
Crashes and sirens, be-bop pretenders
Horning bird tunes
In the slap-slap tambourine night where
Howling wolf-dogs and one-eyed
Alley cats
Chase rats bigger than they are.

A kind of blue moon on a lazy sun Ra
Eve precedes midnight,
Round midnight, Georgia on my mind
And you
Stepped out of a wet-dream and left
My heart in
San Francisco on a train to Harlem.

Funk, blue funk, up-tempo funk;
Yodel-yodel do

Funking with count who?
Yodel-yodel do
Funking with count who?

Miles and miles ahead smoke gets
In your eyes
When autumn leaves fall, burn and
Cannonball is somewhere over the rainbow
Smoking something else
On a Trane where love is supreme.

She's in the nude for love, but sometimes
Jimmy feels like
A motherless child walking up and down
On Green Dolphin Street
Near Leo's Blue Note Club where Jug
Did it his way
Leaving Dex to finger-funk those big
Shiny stockings...
My favorite things.

On the red-vested turntable lady day
Blesses the child
That's got his own cause it might
As well be spring
When there's jazz in the morning, moaning
And moving
Fingers stroking elephant tusk.

Edie B. is spinning funkology for wives and
Lovers who need
That prelude to a kiss before they
Thang
A sophisticated lady and never let
Her go.

The creator has a master plan for every
Spider Burking man
Jamming a Sunday kind of love with
A salad of singers—

Sassy and King Pleasure too, dash in
Some Ella; Johnny, Leon, and Dinah
So blue…. Call
Ceora; tell her that jazz and life are on
The street where
Lee lives … big-booty
Ave., East St. Louis Toodle OO!
Um-Um-Um at the end of a life affair.

MILES DEWEY DAVIS: 1926-1991

(A friend of my mom and dad)

Take a soul-Trane with Miles as he
Rains fresh
Water for a dry soul, melodies that
Make love
To you in tones brazen and blue
In tones
So Miles Davis soft and new

Ride with Miles to west of the mountains
Kilimanjaro and east
Of river Gambia—he will spit you
A lullaby that forms rainbows in the
Night sky

And build you a dream
Of harmonious
Bluesy notes parading magically,
Resonating
In your soul—muted—gently from
That horny trumpet kissing his
Puckered lips.

KATHERINE DUNHAM: 1911-2008

(For a grand lady that taught me a lot)

Katherine's mission was to be
At center stage
In East St. Louis, IL, making it
The world's center
At ninety-six, Dumballah's daughter ascended
To star
On an eternal stage, our leggy Fulani
Queen joined
Papa Legba's Ile.

We have a goddess to fend for us:
Awaken the drum-gods
Shake the rattle spirits
Raise the skirts
Flash the thighs
Kick up the dust
Shout, sing, dance, and celebrate—
Mama Dunham
Premiers at a gathering of souls.

SEEN AND NOT SEEN

Soul is ... the substance of all things
Hoped for
The creator and provider of all
Things seen
And not seen; it's the beginning
And the end
The dark and the light

The cause and the effect, the in
And the out
The wealth and the money
The up and down

The front and back
Body and soul
Beauty and beast
Provider and provisions

The seed and the fruit
Creator and created
Thought and thing
Bird and sky

Sender and receiver
Sound and silence
Over and under
Sweet and sour

Wet and dry
Ship and sea
Storm and calm
Lightning and thunder

Whole and parts
Large and small
One and many
Question and answer
Known and unknown

Life and afterlife
Soul is ... all there is,
Was, or ever will be

W H O L E
It's soul that shelters from winter's
Cold
Binding in with out making life
Whole

Soul labors bringing us gold
Enriching human
Lives willing us bold
Soul
Is persistent pursuing our
Goals
Weaving bountiful dreams and
Bidding them unfold

Soul is timeless, never growing
Old—binding
In with out making life whole.

THE GIVER

Travel from star to star
You will likely travel
Very far
Zero to infinity
Could never measure
Serenity
Trek the universe
End to end
You'll never find the sea
Where life begins
Its harmony so divine
And sweet
With gifts for all—wrapped
Nice and neat.

CONTROL

(For those who don't know why the army, police, and church exist)

Think what I tell
You to
Think, believe what
I tell you
To believe, learn what
I tell you
To learn, know what
I tell you
To know, and do what
I tell you
To do—said the conqueror
To the captive.

BLACK-TASTIC GENIUS

From whence cometh
The genius
Of humankind; what
Endless river of knowledge
Flows into
The sea of our mind?

Endowing us with conscious
Creative intelligence,
Kissing us softly with the lips
Of truth,
Lifting us above prisons
Of ignorance
Into an infinite universe of
Omnipotent erudition.

From whence cometh the genius
In humans? What
Boundless vision of self can
We conceive?

Let us like a crayfish scuttle
Backwards across
The hills and valleys of immeasurable
Time to find
The eternal essence of self where
All there is
Was, all there will be is.

Know that self is whole and
It conjures juju
Magic to manifest all it needs
Incessantly.
Now, like James "The Godfather" Brown,
Let us loudly
Declare: I've got soul and I'm
Superbad.

ALAH DE = GOD IS

God is:
A cloudy sky
A happy guy
A butterfly
Taste of honey
Endless money
Always quite funny

A bumble bee
A Mango tree
A being that's free
A mountain high
A chicken thigh
A buzzing housefly

A hummingbird
A mountain-goat herd
A kind and gentle word
A bright shiny star
A brand-new car
A pickle jar

A special wish
A tasty dish
A fish
A waterfall
A telephone call
God is—one and all
IF ONLY

Flashes of greatness,
Pearls of
Wisdom, riches beyond
Measure,
Perfection of body and
Mind with
Eternity of being
Deemed
Delusions of grandeur some

Authorities say.
If only the dreamer knew
Dreams
Are spiritual seeds, realities
That can come
True
And lift the dreamer beyond
The blue.
If only the dreamer knew.

WITHOUT HANDS

Without hands, soul created worlds
Without end,
Wealth without limit, and thought
Beyond measure

Manifested a world, giving rivers
A trail to run,
Plants to sprout, and bear fruit

One potent soul-life giving life
And form to all:
Including horned hooves on mountains
High
And slithering creatures in forest valleys

Humans, in a variety of shapes, colors,
Sizes—given hands
To build inspired dreams incessantly

To walk tall and stroll proud in this
Universe of wonders,
Walk tall and stroll proud in this
Universe of abundance,
Walk tall and stroll proud in this
Universe of truth

Walk tall and stroll proud in this
Universe of love,
Walk tall and stroll proud in this
Universe of mind,
Vibrant and conscious of self—
Centered
In soul's eternal being.

PROVISIONS

There is a place
To suckle
For all who
Hunger
In our God-given
Universe.

WHERE IS THE GOD-SOUL?

(For Henry Randolph/aka, Akinri Mola 1948-2013)

Query the universe; it will
Respond—
Uniquely, profoundly.
Two friends sit admiring
Lightning
Flashes snaking silently in
Skies
Above distant hills where
Rain
Clouds puffed and swollen
March
Like robotic soldiers as they
Move
Swiftly towards the inquisitive
Friends
Rain descends, grasses and
Plants
Are drummed as rain
Parades
Over the hills and valley
Leaves and root systems
Drink
Deeply and lie in mud after the
Deluge
Swarming insects rise from
Beneath
Water-drunk foliage flushed
Clean
From pounding tropical rain
Wings
Swoop and begin to feast, two
Friends
Bear witness to the might and
Majesty
Of forces seen and not seen; the

Universe
Has responded to their query.
Where
 Is the God-soul? Everywhere
Seen
And not seen, binding in
With out
Making life one grand eternal
Whole.

LESSON # 005

There is the truth of
God
And the truth of
Humans
In due season
God
Reveals it is the truth of
Humans
We must endeavor to
Unravel.

ON GUARD

Humans have become
Experts
At infusing truth with
Fiction
Confusing and deceiving
Those
Who cannot discern one
From the other.

LIKES AND DISLIKES

The individual manifested by its
Soul-self
Is a model of perfection to not
Be compared to
Other models of its kind-kin
One perfect model
Of each human being or
Thing
No two are alike and any
Judgement
As to one model being more
Perfect
Than another is arbitrary and biased.

DRUGGED

Once you have been
 Exposed
To truth, you
Will never be the
Same;
Truth is an addictive
Drug
That will consume
YOU.

THE LAST DIASPORIC AFRICAN

(For sister Juliet Ryan—founder of Blaxit)

Where will you be when
The last African
Repatriates back to the
Motherland
And is no longer feeling like
A motherless child?
Will you be rejoicing with the
Living
Who are bearing witness or will
You bear witness
With the ancestors as they shed
Tears
Of joy that will make Africa's deserts
Lush and rich
With vegetation on that day?

WHO BE FREE?

In America:
If you be black—
The only way
Up—is out.

KWANSABA FOR TONI
MORRISON — 1931 - 2019

(In remembrance of the brunch she had with Gene and me)

As a pioneer at Random House, sister
Toni built bridges for brother Eugene Redmond
To carry Henry Dumas' *ARK OF BONES*
To *SPIRITS KNOWN AND UNKNOWN*. Toni built
Bridges to uplift souls so they could
Discern the PIECES that make them who
They are and relish being truly BELOVED.

Lightning Source UK Ltd.
Milton Keynes UK
UKHW011022051220
374661UK00001B/210